I0410238

WEALTHFLOW: A JOURNEY TO FINANCIAL FREEDOM

Daniel D. Sims

All rights reserved. No part of this publication may be reproduced, redistributed, or transmitted in any form or in any means, including photocopying, recording, or other electronic or mechanical method, without the prior written permission of the publisher, except in the case of brief quotations embodied in critical reviews and certain other non-commercial uses permitted by copyright law.

Copyright © (Daniel D. Sims), (2023)

CHAPTER 1	**4**
CHAPTER 2	**9**
CHAPTER 3	**15**
CHAPTER 4	**21**
CHAPTER 5	**27**
CHAPTER 6	**33**
CHAPTER 7	**39**

CHAPTER 1

INTRODUCTION TO WEALTHFLOW

Wealthflow is an idea that typifies the powerful development of monetary assets inside a person's or an association's monetary biological system.

A basic part of monetary administration centers around how cash is procured, made due, contributed, and used to accomplish long haul monetary objectives.

In this complete investigation, we will dive into the complexities of wealthflow, its importance, and its effect on monetary prosperity.

What is Wealthflow?

Wealthflow, frequently alluded to as the "progression of riches," incorporates the whole lifecycle of cash inside a monetary framework.

It incorporates different parts like pay, costs, reserve funds, ventures, obligation to the board, and abundance protection.

Understanding wealthflow is fundamental for anybody looking for monetary soundness, autonomy, and success.

The Parts of Wealthflow

Pay: The underpinning of wealthflow starts with the inflow of cash, basically through procured pay.This pay can emerge from different sources, including work, business proprietorship, speculations, or investment properties.
The consistency and measure of pay assume a huge part in deciding one's wealthflow.

Expenses: Overseeing costs is essential in keeping a solid wealthflow.
It includes planning and controlling spending to guarantee that pay surpasses or if nothing else approaches consumptions.
Diminishing superfluous costs can let loose assets for saving and financial planning, decidedly influencing wealthflow.

Savings: Reserve funds are an essential component of wealthflow.

Cash saved today can be contributed and developed after some time, adding to future abundance.

Laying out a reserve fund's propensity is an imperative move toward building monetary security.

Investments: Giving cash something to do through speculations is a vital driver of wealthflow.

Ventures can incorporate stocks, securities, land, common assets, from there, the sky's the limit.

The objective is to create returns that surpass the pace of expansion and duties, accordingly expanding by and large abundance.

Obligation The executives: Overseeing and paying off past commitments is fundamental for a sound wealthflow.

Exorbitant interest obligations can deplete monetary assets and obstruct abundance amassing.

Successful obligation the board systems can speed up the excursion toward independence from the rat race.

Abundance Protection: Shielding aggregated abundance from unanticipated occasions is vital. Protection, domain arranging, and resource insurance procedures guarantee that abundance stays in salvageable shape and can be passed down to people in the future.

The Meaning of Wealthflow

Understanding wealthflow isn't just about collecting abundance; it's tied in with accomplishing monetary security and chasing after one's monetary objectives successfully.

Here are a few key justifications for why wealthflow matters:

1. Monetary Soundness

A very much oversaw wealthflow guarantees that you have a stable monetary base.

It permits you to cover your everyday costs, crises, and startling expenses without depending on obligation.

Monetary solidness gives inner serenity and decreases pressure.

2. Abundance Gathering

Wealthflow is the cycle through which abundance gathers after some time.

By streamlining your monetary choices and speculations, you can speed up abundance development and work toward accomplishing your monetary objectives, whether that is retirement, homeownership, or monetary freedom.

3. Monetary Freedom

Wealthflow is a pathway to monetary freedom.

At the point when your automated revenue (from speculations) surpasses your costs, you have accomplished independence from the rat race.

You never again need to depend exclusively on procured pay, giving you the adaptability to seek after your interests and interests.

4. Inheritance Building

Wealthflow stretches out past your lifetime.

Appropriate home arranging guarantees that your abundance is passed down to your main beneficiaries or assigned recipients.

This heritage can give open doors and monetary security to people in the future.

Procedures for Enhancing Wealthflow

To improve your wealthflow, consider embracing the accompanying systems:

1. Planning

Making a point by point financial plan permits you to follow your pay and costs.

It distinguishes regions where you can reduce expenses and designate more assets toward reserve funds and ventures.

2. Secret stash

Assemble a secret stash to cover unforeseen costs.

Having a monetary security net guarantees that surprising difficulties don't upset your wealthflow.

3. Obligation Decrease
Focus on settling exorbitant interest obligations.
As you pay off past commitments, a greater amount of your pay can be directed into reserve funds and ventures.

4. Enhanced Ventures
Enhance your venture portfolio to spread risk.
Think about a blend of stocks, bonds, land, and other resource classes to enhance returns.

5. Nonstop Learning
Remain informed about individual accounting and venture procedures.
Instruction engages you to go with informed choices and adjust to changing monetary scenes.

6. Proficient Direction

Look for guidance from monetary consultants or experts who can give customized techniques in light of your monetary objectives and conditions.

Conclusion

All in all, wealthflow is the heartbeat of monetary achievement.

It's about the amount you acquire, yet how actually you make due, save, contribute, and safeguard your cash.

By understanding the parts of wealthflow and carrying out sound monetary systems, people and associations can accomplish more prominent monetary security, autonomy, and success.

Recall that wealthflow is a unique cycle that requires progressing consideration and flexibility, however the prizes it offers as far as monetary prosperity are certainly worth the endeavors

CHAPTER 2

GRASPING MONETARY PREPARATION

Monetary arranging is a central part of dealing with one's monetary assets, accomplishing monetary objectives, and getting a steady and prosperous future. A far reaching process includes setting goals, assessing current monetary status, and creating methodologies to meet those targets. In this investigation, we will dive into the complexities of monetary preparation, its significance, key parts, and moves toward making a powerful monetary arrangement.

The Significance of Monetary Preparation

Monetary arranging assumes a crucial part in a person's or an association's monetary prosperity. It gives a guide to overseeing funds effectively and pursuing informed monetary choices. Here are a few convincing motivations behind why understanding monetary arranging is vital:

1. Objective Accomplishment

Monetary arranging helps people characterize and focus on their monetary objectives, whether it's purchasing a home, putting something aside for retirement, or subsidizing a youngster's schooling. It gives an organized way to deal with pursuing these goals.

2. Planning and Cost Control

A basic part of monetary arranging is planning. It permits people to follow pay and costs, guaranteeing that spending lines up with monetary objectives. It recognizes regions where cost-cutting is conceivable, opening up assets for reserve funds and ventures.

3. Risk The executives
Monetary arranging implies evaluating and relieving monetary dangers. This can incorporate techniques, for example, protection inclusion to safeguard against unexpected occasions like ailment, mishaps, or property harm.

4. Abundance Gathering
By making a monetary arrangement, people can recognize valuable chances to contribute and develop their riches. It helps in enhancing speculation choices to accomplish better yields while overseeing risk.

5. Retirement Arranging

Understanding monetary arranging is fundamental for retirement readiness. It assists people with deciding the amount they need to put something aside for retirement and select proper speculation methodologies to accomplish their retirement pay objectives.

6. Monetary Security

A thoroughly examined monetary arrangement gives monetary security, guaranteeing that people have assets set up to deal with crises and surprising costs without depending on obligation.

Key Parts of Monetary Preparation

Monetary arranging comprises of a few key parts that all in all structure a thorough procedure for overseeing funds successfully:

1. Putting forth Monetary Objectives

The groundwork of monetary arranging starts with defining clear and reachable monetary objectives. These objectives can be present moment (e.g., taking care of charge card obligation), mid-term (e.g., purchasing a home), or long haul (e.g., retirement arranging).

2. Surveying Monetary Circumstance

A significant stage in understanding monetary arranging is assessing one's ongoing monetary status. This incorporates dissecting pay, costs, resources, liabilities, and total assets. It gives a standard to making a monetary arrangement.

3. Planning and Income The executives

Planning includes making a definite arrangement for money and costs. It assists people with dispensing assets for different necessities, like lodging, transportation, food, and amusement, while guaranteeing that reserve funds and speculations are focused on.

4. Risk Appraisal

Recognizing and it is fundamental to evaluate monetary dangers. This incorporates assessing takes a chance connected with wellbeing, property, pay, and ventures. Fitting gamble the board methodologies, like protection, are then executed.

5. Speculation Arranging
Speculation arranging includes deciding how to dispense assets among various venture vehicles, like stocks, securities, land, and bank accounts. The objective is to accomplish ideal returns while overseeing risk.

6. Charge Arranging
Understanding the expense ramifications of monetary choices is significant. Charge arranging systems plan to limit charge obligation while amplifying after-government forms on speculations and pay.

7. Retirement Arranging
Getting ready for retirement is a huge part of monetary preparation. It includes working out retirement needs, laying out retirement accounts (e.g., 401(k), IRA), and fostering a methodology to accomplish wanted retirement pay.

8. Domain Arranging

Domain arranging guarantees that resources are conveyed by one's desires in the afterlife. It incorporates making wills, trusts, and appointing recipients for monetary records.

Moves toward Make a Viable Monetary Arrangement

Making a successful monetary arrangement requires an organized methodology. Here are the fundamental stages to foster an exhaustive monetary arrangement:

1. Characterize Monetary Objectives

Begin by recognizing and focusing on monetary objectives. Decide if they are present moment, mid-term, or long haul objectives. Be explicit and reasonable about what you need to accomplish.

2. Assess Current Monetary Status

Assemble all pertinent monetary data, including pay, costs, resources, and liabilities. Compute your total assets to grasp your ongoing monetary position.

3. Make a Financial plan
Foster a definite financial plan that frames your pay and costs. Allot assets to various cost classes, leaving space for reserve funds and speculations.

4. Foster a Gamble The executives Procedure
Recognize possible monetary dangers and foster methodologies to alleviate them. This might incorporate buying insurance contracts, like wellbeing, life, or property protection.

5. Venture Arranging
Decide your gamble resistance and speculation objectives. Dispense assets among various speculation choices in view of your gamble profile and goals.

6. Charge Arranging

Think about charge productive speculation methodologies and investigate charge saving open doors, for example, adding to retirement accounts or using tax reductions.

7. Retirement Arranging
Compute your retirement needs and make an arrangement to accomplish your retirement pay objectives. Consider factors like Government backed retirement benefits, annuity plans, and venture returns.

8. Domain Arranging
On the off chance that pertinent, make or update your request plan. This incorporates drafting a will, assigning recipients, and taking into account procedures to limit home charges.

9. Carry out and Screen
Set your monetary strategy in motion and consistently screen your advancement. Change your arrangement on a case by case basis to oblige changes in your monetary circumstance or objectives.

10. Look for Proficient Direction

Consider counseling a confirmed monetary organizer or counselor to help you make and deal with your monetary arrangement. They can give aptitude and direction custom-made to your particular conditions.

Conclusion

Understanding monetary arranging is fundamental for accomplishing monetary security, creating financial stability, and understanding your monetary objectives. A dynamic and progressing process adjusts to life's progressions and developing monetary scenes. By following the critical parts and steps framed in this investigation, people and associations can make successful monetary plans that prepare for a prosperous and monetarily secure future.

CHAPTER 3

BUILDING A STRONG MONETARY ESTABLISHMENT

Monetary solidness and security are the foundations of a prosperous and effortless future. Building a strong monetary establishment isn't just a reasonable decision however a basic need in the present consistently changing financial scene. In this exhaustive conversation, we will investigate the key standards, systems, and steps engaged with laying out an unshakable monetary establishment.

The Significance of a Solid Monetary Establishment

A strong monetary establishment fills in as the bedrock whereupon an individual or a family can fabricate their monetary future. It gives dependability, strength, and genuine serenity even with monetary difficulties and open doors. Here's the reason it's critical:

1. Monetary Security

A solid monetary establishment guarantees that you can cover your fundamental requirements and handle startling costs without depending on using a credit card or draining your investment funds. This security is fundamental for an inward feeling of harmony.

2. Opportunity and Decision

Monetary solidness opens ways to amazing open doors and gives you decisions throughout everyday life. Whether it's chasing after advanced education, beginning a business, or partaking in an agreeable retirement, a strong monetary establishment gives the necessary resources to make these fantasies a reality.

3. Obligation The executives
A solid monetary base permits you to really oversee and pay off past commitments. You can stay away from the pattern of collecting exorbitant interest obligations by having the assets to settle existing advances.

4. Speculation and Establishing long term financial stability
With a strong monetary establishment, you can dispense more assets toward speculations that develop your abundance after some time. This can incorporate stocks, securities, land, and retirement accounts.

5. Monetary Freedom
Accomplishing monetary freedom, where your automated revenue surpasses your costs, is a critical achievement. It awards you the opportunity to seek after your inclinations and interests without being attached to a check.

Standards of Building a Strong Monetary Establishment

Building a strong monetary establishment includes sticking to key rules that guide your monetary choices and activities. These standards structure the premise of sound monetary administration:

1. Planning

Making and adhering to a spending plan is basic. It assists you with following your pay and costs, guaranteeing that you live inside your means and have excess assets for saving and effective money management.

2. Secret stash

Laying out a secret stash is a basic step. This save of money covers startling costs, for example, hospital expenses or vehicle fixes, without upsetting your monetary soundness.

3. Obligation The board

Focus on settling exorbitant premium obligations, beginning with Visas and advances with exorbitant financing costs. Paying off past commitments permits you to divert assets toward reserve funds and speculations.

4. Saving
Normal saving is fundamental for building a monetary establishment. It gives a pad to future requirements and valuable open doors. Save a piece of your pay reliably, regardless of whether it's a modest quantity.

5. Venture
Venture is a vital driver of establishing a strong financial foundation. Apportion assets to different speculation vehicles in light of your gamble resilience and long haul objectives. Broadening oversees risk.

6. Protection
Protection defends your monetary establishment against startling occasions. Guarantee you have satisfactory inclusion for wellbeing, life,

inability, and property to moderate likely monetary misfortunes.

7. Retirement Arranging

Plan for retirement early. Add to retirement accounts like 401(k)s or IRAs to get your monetary future. Consider counseling a monetary guide to upgrade your retirement methodology.

Moves toward Construct a Strong Monetary Establishment

Building a strong monetary establishment requires a methodical methodology. Here are the fundamental stages to assist you with getting everything rolling:

1. Survey What is going on

Start by assessing your monetary status. Work out your total assets by deducting your liabilities from your resources. Audit your pay, costs, and obligation commitments.

2. Put forth Clear Monetary Objectives

Characterize your monetary objectives, both present moment and long haul. Your objectives will direct your monetary choices and assist you with remaining propelled.

3. Make a Financial plan
Foster a reasonable spending plan that frames your pay and costs. Guarantee that your costs don't surpass your pay and allot assets for saving and effective financial planning.

4. Assemble a Rainy day account
Begin putting something aside for crises. Expect to save no less than three to a half year of everyday costs in a promptly open record.

5. Tackle Exorbitant Interest Obligation
Center around squaring away exorbitant interest obligations forcefully. This might include making additional installments or uniting advances to bring down loan costs.

6. Save Reliably

Lay out a propensity for ordinary saving. Robotize your reserve funds by setting up programmed moves to your investment funds or speculation accounts.

7. Contribute Shrewdly

Enhance your ventures in view of your gamble resilience and objectives. Consider counseling a monetary guide for customized venture techniques.

8. Acquire Satisfactory Protection

Audit your protection inclusion to guarantee it addresses your issues. Make changes as the need should arise, like expanding inclusion or adding strategies.

9. Plan for Retirement

Add to retirement records and exploit business supported plans like 401(k)s. Decide your retirement pay objectives and change your commitments as needs be.

10. Persistently Instruct Yourself

Remain informed about individual accounting and speculation subjects. Information enables you to go with informed monetary choices.

11. Look for Proficient Direction

Consider counseling a confirmed monetary organizer or guide for customized monetary exhortation and procedures.

Difficulties and Barriers

Building a strong monetary establishment can be testing, particularly even with surprising misfortunes or financial slumps. Here are a few normal provokes and systems to beat them:

1. Pay Vacillations

In the event that your pay vacillates, make a financial plan that records for both high and low-pay months. Construct a monetary pad during prosperous times to cover costs during lean months.

2. Startling Costs

Set up a secret stash to deal with startling costs. In the event that a critical unforeseen expense emerges, investigate choices like low-premium individual credits as opposed to depending on exorbitant premium charge cards.

3. Obligation Overpower

On the off chance that you have a significant obligation, consider obligation combination or obligation on the board plans. Look for help from credit advising offices to arrange lower financing costs or reimbursement terms.

4. Absence of Discipline

Keeping up with monetary discipline can be challenging. Consider utilizing planning applications, robotizing reserve funds, or enrolling a responsibility accomplice to remain focused.

Conclusion

Building a strong monetary establishment is certainly not a short-term accomplishment yet a long lasting excursion. It requires discipline, arranging, and responsibility. The advantages of monetary security, strength, and the capacity to seek after your fantasies far offset the work and forfeits required. By sticking to the standards and steps illustrated in this conversation and staying versatile even with monetary difficulties, you can build a strong monetary establishment that upholds your objectives and goals into the indefinite future.

CHAPTER 4

CONTRIBUTING FOR ABUNDANCE DEVELOPMENT

Contributing is an amazing asset for abundance development and monetary thriving. It permits people and associations to give their cash something to do, producing returns and expanding their total assets over the long haul. In this thorough investigation, we will dig into the complexities of money management for abundance development, examining the significance of financial planning, different venture choices, techniques, and key standards to prevail in the realm of speculation.

The Significance of Effective financial planning for Abundance Development

Contributing is something other than a method for saving riches; it is a pathway to huge abundance development. Here are a few convincing motivations behind why contributing is significant for people and associations looking for monetary flourishing:

1. Abundance Aggregation

Contributing permits people to develop their abundance after some time. Rather than allowing cash to sit inactive, speculations can possibly produce returns, which can compound and prompt significant abundance gathering.

2. Beat Expansion

Expansion disintegrates the buying influence of cash over the long run. Putting resources into resources that dominate expansion safeguards the genuine worth of your abundance and guarantees your cash keeps on working for you.

3. Accomplish Monetary Objectives

Contributing is a critical instrument for accomplishing monetary objectives like purchasing a home, financing a kid's schooling, or resigning easily. It gives the valuable chance to produce the expected assets by procuring a profit from speculations.

4. Pay Age
Numerous speculations turn out normal revenue as profits, interest, or rental pay. This can enhance acquired pay and work on generally speaking monetary solidness.

5. Enhancement
Contributing offers enhancement benefits. By spreading speculations across various resource classes, people can decrease risk and accomplish a more adjusted and stable portfolio.

Different Venture Choices
There are different venture choices accessible to people and associations, each with its own qualities and hazard bring profiles back. Here are some normal speculation choices:

1. Stocks

Stocks address proprietorship in an organization and proposition the potential for capital appreciation. Financial backers purchase portions of stock with the assumption that their worth will increment over the long haul. Stocks can be unpredictable however offer the potential for significant yields.

2. Bonds

Securities are obligation protections gave by state run administrations, companies, or regions. They pay intermittent interest (coupon) and return the chief sum at development. Bonds are by and large considered lower risk than stocks however offer lower likely returns.

3. Land

Land speculations include buying actual properties like private or business land. Land can turn out rental revenue and value in esteem after some time.

4. Common Assets

Common supports pool cash from numerous financial backers to put resources into a differentiated arrangement of stocks, bonds, or different protections. They offer enhancement and expert administration.

5. Trade Exchanged Assets (ETFs)

ETFs are like common assets however exchange on stock trades like individual stocks. They give liquidity and enhancement, frequently with lower expenses than common assets.

6. Products

Financial backers can put resources into wares like gold, silver, oil, and rural items. These speculations can go about as supports against expansion and market instability.

7. Digital forms of money

Digital forms of money like Bitcoin and Ethereum have acquired prevalence as elective speculations. They are exceptionally unstable however have the potential for huge returns.

8. Retirement Records

Retirement accounts like 401(k)s and IRAs offer expense benefits for long haul retirement investment funds. They frequently incorporate an assortment of speculation choices.

Venture Procedures for Abundance Development

Contributing for abundance development requires insightful preparation and key direction. Here are some venture techniques to consider:

1. Long haul Money management

Long haul money management includes holding resources for a lengthy period, regularly years or many years. It permits ventures to profit from intensifying returns and brave market unpredictability.

2. Mitigating risk over time

Mitigating risk implies routinely effective financial planning, a decent measure of cash, and paying little mind to economic situations. This procedure can lessen the effect of market vacillations and below normal expense of speculations over the long haul.

3. Resource Designation

Resource designation includes spreading ventures across various resource classes (e.g., stocks, bonds, land) to accomplish a harmony among chance and return. The portion ought to line up with a financial backer's gamble resistance and monetary objectives.

4. Broadening

Broadening speculations across different resources and ventures can lessen risk. It keeps the whole portfolio from being unfavorably impacted by the terrible showing of solitary speculation.

5. Risk The executives

Understanding and overseeing risk is fundamental for effective contributing. This incorporates surveying risk resistance, differentiating speculations, and setting stop-misfortune orders to restrict expected misfortunes.

6. Research and An expected level of investment

Intensive exploration and an expected level of effort are basic prior to pursuing speculation choices. Financial backers ought to evaluate the basics of the speculation, the history of the resource, and any related dangers.

7. Proficient Direction

Numerous financial backers look for guidance from monetary counselors or speculation experts. A certified counselor can give customized venture methodologies and direction in view of a person's monetary circumstance and objectives.

Key Standards for Fruitful Financial planning

Fruitful financial planning is based on an underpinning of key rules that guide independent direction and portfolio the board. Here are a few fundamental standards to remember:

1. Begin Early
The force of intensifying works best after some time. Beginning to contribute early can essentially support abundance development.

2. Put forth Clear Objectives
Characterize clear and explicit venture objectives. Having an unmistakable reason for your ventures helps in navigation.

3. Remain Informed
Remain informed about market patterns, financial turns of events, and changes in venture systems. Information is an important resource in the realm of money management.

4. Persistence and Discipline

Contributing frequently includes market changes and periodic slumps. Persistence and discipline are critical to keep with it during testing times.

5. Survey and Change

Consistently audit your speculation portfolio and change it depending on the situation to line up with your objectives and hazard resistance. Rebalance your portfolio to keep up with your ideal resource designation.

6. Stay away from Profound Independent direction

Profound choices, driven by dread or ravenousness, can prompt unfortunate venture results. Adhere to your speculation technique and try not to pursue hasty choices.

Conclusion

Contributing for abundance development is a principal procedure for accomplishing monetary thriving and getting one's monetary future. It gives the chance to produce returns, beat expansion, and accomplish monetary objectives.

Grasping the significance of effective financial planning, investigating different speculation choices, carrying out viable venture systems, and sticking to scratch standards are basic parts of fruitful abundance development through speculations. By adopting a proactive and informed strategy to effective money management, people and associations can outfit the capability of the monetary business sectors to create enduring financial wellbeing and monetary security.

CHAPTER 5

OVERSEEING AND SAFEGUARDING YOUR RICHES

Riches, once obtained, require cautious administration and assurance to guarantee its life span and handiness in accomplishing monetary objectives. Compelling abundance the board includes methodologies for developing, protecting, and decisively using one's resources. In this complete investigation, we will dig into the complexities of overseeing and safeguarding your abundance, examining the significance of abundance on the board, key parts, techniques, and best practices to shield your monetary prosperity.

The Significance of Overseeing and Safeguarding Riches

Abundance of the board isn't restricted to high-total assets people; it is a basic part of monetary prosperity for everybody. Here are a few convincing justifications for why overseeing and it is significant to safeguard your riches:

1. Long haul Monetary Security

Successful abundance the board guarantees that you have the assets and monetary dependability to address your issues and objectives over the long haul. It gives a wellbeing net in the midst of financial vulnerability or individual emergencies.

2. Objective Accomplishment
Abundance the board adjusts your monetary assets to your objectives. Whether it's purchasing a home, financing training, or resigning serenely, a very much organized abundance the executives plan assists you with accomplishing these goals.

3. Inheritance Conservation
For some, abundance isn't only for individual use; helping people in the future is likewise planned. Legitimate administration and insurance of abundance guarantee that it very well may be passed down to beneficiaries or worthy missions, leaving an enduring inheritance.

4. Alleviating Dangers
Successful abundance the executives incorporates risk appraisal and moderation. It includes techniques like protection and resource

insurance to safeguard your abundance from unanticipated occasions and liabilities.

5. Charge Proficiency

Abundance the executives incorporates charge wanting to limit the effect of expenses on your resources. Vital duty arranging can streamline your monetary results and safeguard your abundance from pointless disintegration.

Key Parts of Abundance The board

Abundance the board includes different parts that together structure an exhaustive procedure for overseeing and safeguarding your monetary assets:

1. Monetary Preparation

Monetary arranging is the groundwork of abundance on the board. It includes laying out clear monetary objectives, evaluating what is going on, making spending plans, and creating techniques to accomplish your goals.

2. Speculation The board

Speculation the board includes choosing and overseeing ventures to advance returns while overseeing risk. It incorporates resource distribution, portfolio broadening, and continuous observation of speculation execution.

3. Risk The board
Risk the board surveys and mitigates expected dangers to your riches, including protection inclusion, home preparation, and legitimate procedures to safeguard resources.

4. Charge Arranging
Charge arranging includes organizing your funds to limit charge liabilities. Procedures incorporate duty proficient speculations, allowances, and credits to decrease the effect of assessments on your abundance.

5. Retirement Arranging
Retirement arranging guarantees that you have satisfactory assets to keep up with your ideal way of life during retirement. It incorporates

working out retirement needs, picking retirement accounts, and laying out pay sources.

6. **Domain Arranging**
Domain arranging includes making an arrangement for the conveyance of resources after your demise. It incorporates wills, trusts, and other lawful instruments to guarantee your abundance is appropriated by your desires.

7. **Income The board**
Income the board centers around enhancing the inflow and outpouring of cash. It incorporates planning, following costs, and guaranteeing that money is accessible for fundamental requirements and open doors.

8. **Resource Assurance**
Resource assurance procedures protect your abundance from banks, claims, and unexpected occasions. These may incorporate lawful designs like trusts and the utilization of protection items.

Methodologies for Overseeing and Safeguarding Your Riches

Actually overseeing and safeguarding your abundance includes the execution of key methodologies and best practices. Here are a few vital systems to consider:

1. Expand Speculations

Expansion includes spreading your speculations across various resource classes and enterprises to decrease risk. A very much expanded portfolio can endure market vacillations.

2. Routinely Audit and Rebalance

Occasionally audit your speculation portfolio and change it on a case by case basis to keep up with your ideal resource distribution. Rebalancing guarantees that your speculations line up with your gamble resilience and monetary objectives.

3. Just-in-case account

Keep a just-in-case account with adequate assets to cover startling costs or monetary misfortunes.

A backup stash gives a monetary security net, lessening the need to plunge into ventures during emergencies.

4. Protection Inclusion

Assess your protection needs, including wellbeing, life, incapacity, and obligation protection. Sufficient protection inclusion shields your abundance from unforeseen occasions.

5. Bequest Arranging

Make a far reaching home arrangement that frames your desires for resource circulation. Talk with lawful experts to guarantee that your domain plan is legitimately strong and charge effective.

6. Proficient Direction

Think about looking for counsel from monetary guides, domain organizers, and assessment experts. These specialists can give customized methodologies in view of your one of a kind monetary circumstance and objectives.

7. Charge Proficiency

Streamline your monetary choices for charge productivity. This incorporates utilizing charge advantaged accounts, charge proficient speculations, and duty saving methodologies to limit your expense responsibility.

8. Remain Informed

Remain informed about monetary business sectors, financial patterns, and changes in charge regulations. Information engages you to settle on informed choices and adjust your abundance of the board systems depending on the situation.

Best Practices for Abundance The executives

Abundance of the executives is a continuous cycle that requires tirelessness and consideration. Here are a few prescribed procedures to guarantee viable abundance the board:

1. Put forth Clear Objectives

Characterize explicit and attainable monetary objectives. Having clear goals directs your abundance of board choices.

2. Keep up with Records

Keep coordinated records of monetary exchanges, ventures, and significant archives. This improves monetary preparation and works with home organization.

3. Speak with Family

Examine your abundance of board plans and bequest aims with your relatives. Open correspondence can forestall misconceptions and clashes later on.

4. Intermittent Surveys

Consistently survey your abundance of the executives methodologies and make changes on a case by case basis. Changes in private conditions or monetary objectives might expect alterations to your arrangement.

5. Stay away from Rash Choices

Abstain from going with rash monetary choices, particularly during market instability. Adhere to your drawn out abundance of the board plan.

6. Teach Yourself

Consistently teach yourself about monetary ideas and venture choices. Information enables you to pursue educated choices and evaluate the counsel regarding monetary experts.

Conclusion

Overseeing and safeguarding your abundance is a complex undertaking that requires cautious preparation, key independent direction, and continuous consideration. By grasping the significance of abundance the board, perceiving the key parts, and carrying out powerful techniques and best practices, people and associations can defend their monetary prosperity and work toward accomplishing their drawn out monetary objectives. Abundance the board isn't just about developing resources; it's tied in with saving and decisively using those resources for upgrading monetary security and making an enduring heritage.

CHAPTER 6

TECHNIQUES FOR MAINTAINABLE WEALTHFLOW

Manageable wealthflow, frequently alluded to as monetary manageability, is the capacity to keep a predictable and solid stream of pay, reserve funds, and ventures over the long haul. Accomplishing practical wealthflow is an objective for people and associations the same, as it gives monetary steadiness, inner serenity, and the ability to seek after monetary objectives and desires. In this complete investigation, we will dig into different procedures that can help you lay out and keep up with manageable wealthflow.

What is Maintainable Wealthflow?

Reasonable wealthflow can be characterized as the reliable age and the board of monetary assets to help one's ideal way of life, monetary objectives, and requirements while saving and developing abundance for what's in store. It's tied in with guaranteeing that you have a solid revenue source, compelling reserve funds and venture rehearses, and the capacity to endure monetary difficulties or unforeseen occasions without undermining your drawn out monetary security.

The Significance of Feasible Wealthflow

For what reason is feasible wealthflow significant? It assumes an essential part in different parts of monetary prosperity:

1. Monetary Dependability

Maintainable wealthflow gives a groundwork of monetary dependability. It guarantees that you have sufficient pay to cover everyday costs, crises, and future objectives, diminishing monetary pressure and tension.

2. Objective Accomplishment

Whether your monetary objectives incorporate homeownership, training for your kids, exiting the workforce, or magnanimous undertakings, economical wealthflow empowers you to pursue these goals without continually stressing over monetary difficulties.

3. Retirement Security
Making arrangements for retirement is a basic part of monetary supportability. Maintainable wealthflow permits you to save and contribute for retirement, guaranteeing that you have adequate pay during your non-working years.

4. Versatility
Life is eccentric, and reasonable wealthflow makes you more versatile to changes in conditions. Whether it's an employment cutback, wellbeing emergency, or monetary slump, having a manageable monetary arrangement set up can assist you with enduring these difficulties.

5. Inheritance Building

For some, supportable wealthflow is about something other than private monetary security. Making a heritage can help people in the future, whether through legacy, beneficent gifts, or different types of monetary help.

Systems for Accomplishing Economical Wealthflow

Accomplishing and keeping up with reasonable wealthflow requires an essential way to deal with dealing with your funds. The following are a few critical procedures to consider:

1. Lay out Clear Monetary Objectives

The underpinning of any practical wealthflow system is characterizing clear and feasible monetary objectives. These objectives can be present moment (e.g., taking care of obligation), mid-term (e.g., purchasing a home), or long haul (e.g., retirement arranging). Having explicit targets gives guidance and inspiration for your monetary endeavors.

2. Make a Point by point Spending plan

Planning is a crucial device for dealing with your funds successfully. It includes following your pay and costs to comprehend where your cash is going. A very much organized financial plan assists you with distributing assets for various necessities, including reserve funds and ventures.

3. Fabricate a Secret stash

A secret stash is a monetary security net that gives genuine serenity and versatility despite unforeseen costs or pay interruptions. Expect to save no less than three to a half year of everyday costs in your secret stash.

4. Center around Obligation The executives

Exorbitant interest obligation can be a critical channel on your funds. Focus on taking care of exorbitant premium obligations, for example, Visa adjusts, to let loose assets for saving and financial planning.

5. Contribute Astutely

Contributing is a vital part of practical wealthflow. Expand your venture portfolio to spread risk, and pick speculations that line up with your monetary objectives and chance resistance. Reliable, long haul money management can assist with developing your riches.

6. Consider Numerous Revenue Sources

Depending exclusively on a solitary type of revenue can be unsafe. Investigate chances to make extra revenue sources, like side organizations, independent work, or automated revenue speculations.

7. Charge Arranging

Improve your expense methodology to limit the effect of assessments on your riches. Consider involving charge advantaged records and look for proficient direction for complex duty arranging.

8. Persistently Instruct Yourself

Monetary proficiency is an important resource in accomplishing feasible wealthflow. Remain informed about individual accounting, venture choices, and monetary techniques. Consistent learning engages you to pursue informed choices.

9. Survey and Change Your Arrangement

Monetary conditions and objectives can change over the long run. Consistently survey your monetary arrangement and make changes on a case by case basis. Adaptability and versatility are fundamental for long haul monetary manageability.

10. Look for Proficient Direction

Monetary counselors and experts can give master guidance and altered techniques in view of your one of a kind monetary circumstance and objectives. Consider talking with an expert to upgrade your wealthflow plan.

Economical Wealthflow Contextual analyses

To outline how practical wealthflow systems can be applied, all things considered, situations, how about we investigate two contextual analyses:

Contextual investigation 1: Retirement Arranging

Alice, matured 45, needs to resign easily at age 65. She lays out a reasonable monetary objective: to aggregate $1 million in retirement reserve funds when she resigns. To accomplish this objective, she:

Makes an itemized financial plan to control expenses and boost investment funds.

Sets up programmed commitments to her retirement accounts every month.

Broadens her venture portfolio to adjust chance and return.

Exploits boss supported retirement plans and expense advantaged retirement accounts.

Audits her retirement plan every year and changes her commitments and speculation methodology depending on the situation.

Through reliable reserve funds and vital money management, Alice is on target to accomplish her retirement objective and keep a reasonable wealthflow in retirement.

Contextual analysis 2: Obligation Decrease

David, matured 35, has aggregated significant Mastercard obligations with exorbitant loan fees. His monetary objective is to become obligation free in five years or less. To accomplish this objective, he:

Makes a spending plan to follow pay and costs.

Dispenses a huge part of his pay to obligation reimbursement.

Focuses on taking care of exorbitant interest Mastercard adjusts first.

Tries not to assume new obligation and utilization bonuses, similar to burden discounts, to make additional installments.

Screens his advancement and celebrates achievements en route.

Through focused obligation decrease, David not just accomplishes his objective of becoming obligation free yet additionally opens up assets for saving and effective financial planning, adding to his manageable wealthflow.

Difficulties to Feasible Wealthflow

While the systems referenced above can help lay out and keep up with supportable wealthflow, there are normal difficulties that people might confront:

1. Financial Slumps

Financial downturns and slumps can influence pay, ventures, and employer stability. Having a monetary arrangement that records for such occasions is urgent.

2. Way of life Expansion

As pay expands, a few people capitulate to way of life expansion, spending more as they procure more. This can prevent investment funds and abundance collection.

3. Absence of Discipline

Keeping up with monetary discipline, particularly when confronted with compulsions to overspend or assume superfluous obligation, can be challenging.

4. Speculation Chance
Contributing consistently conveys some degree of hazard. Market vacillations can influence venture returns, affecting your wealthflow.

5. Wellbeing and Protection
Wellbeing related costs and lacking protection inclusion can upset wealthflow. Satisfactory protection arranging is fundamental.

6. Absence of Monetary Instruction
An absence of monetary information can prompt unfortunate choices and upset long haul monetary maintainability.

Conclusion
Maintainable wealthflow is an attainable objective for the people who are resolved to sound monetary administration practices and

procedures. By putting forth clear monetary objectives, planning, paying off past commitments, contributing shrewdly, and persistently instructing themselves

CHAPTER 7

CONCLUSION

In the outing through the main segments of "Wealthflow," we've explored the versatile components of making due, creating, and supporting overflow. This end segment is the capstone, where we organize the strings of data, experiences, and techniques we've discussed. It's one moment to contemplate the overall guidelines and center focuses that can empower you to graph your own course towards financial accomplishment.

The Wealthflow Framework

All through this book, we've made a wealthflow plan — an aid expected to guide you towards achieving your financial targets and getting a prosperous future. Could we return to the basic parts of this framework:

1. Foundation Building

Wealthflow begins with areas of strength for a. In Segment 3, we complemented the meaning of financial capability, arranging, and commitment of the chiefs. These are the construction blocks whereupon your financial future rests. Without a consistent foundation, the structure of overflow crumbles easily.

2. Imperative Cash the executives

Section 4 introduced key monetary preparation. Overflow doesn't create idly; it requires savvy dispersion of resources into assets that are worth long term. From stocks and land to extended portfolios, the right endeavor methodology can be your overflow's closest friend.

3. Confirmation and Chance Organization

In Segment 5, we discussed the fundamental occupation of chance organization and overflow confirmation. Life is stacked with weaknesses, and safeguarding your overflow against frightening events is a groundwork of financial planning. Assurance, home planning, and emergency saves are your security nets in the stormy waters of life.

4. Reasonability and Advancement

Area 6 examined frameworks for functional wealthflow. Overflow isn't just about social affair assets; it's connected to ensuring they continue on and continue to deliver pay from now onward, indefinitely. Legacy orchestrating, practical hypotheses, and moral thoughts are key pieces of this point.

The Power of Reflection

By and by, in the end, I encourage you to stop briefly to think about your own money-related outing. What have you acquired from this examination of wealthflow? Are there express encounters or procedures that resound with your money related goals and values?

It's fundamental to see that wealthflow is a dynamic, advancing interaction. Comparatively as a stream perpetually changes with its ongoing situation, your financial technique should foster considering developing circumstances. Reliably getting back to your financial game plan, changing your hypotheses, and staying informed about money related designs are exceptionally significant for the trip.

Diagramming Your Course

As we close our examination of wealthflow, review that you are the administrator of your financial boat. You have the data and instruments to investigate the progressions of wealthflow. Your cycle could encounter calm waters and tempestuous seas, yet with an especially made plan and the discipline to comply with it, you can avoid any financial hardships that come your course.

Whether you need to leave calmly, save your children's tutoring, or have a helpful result locally, wealthflow is the asset to achieve those cravings. The capacity to shape your financial future lies in your grip, coordinated by the norms and strategies we've discussed.

Past the Book

While this book fills in as a significant resource, your financial tutoring should never stop. Stay curious, continue to learn, and search for direction from trusted money related specialists when required. Review that overflow isn't just a goal anyway a durable journey — a trip that can be essentially as compensating as the targets you set on the way.

Conclusion: Taking off

With everything taken into account, "Wealthflow" has been your compass in the domain of cash. It's a manual for sorting out the streams and tides of wealth, outfitting you with the gadgets to investigate and thrive. Your money-related trip is an encounter expecting your request, and I encourage you to go out with conviction, reason, and a promise to achieve the wealthflow you need.

May your cycle be stacked up with progress, cleverness, and the fulfillment of your financial dreams. Bon venture!

www.ingramcontent.com/pod-product-compliance
Lightning Source LLC
Chambersburg PA
CBHW062244290526
45794CB00006B/2398